MW01122218

Poetic Thoughts
Of
Schizophrenia

Poetic Thoughts
Of
Schizophrenia

By
Dax Patrick Noden

PUBLISHED BY GOLDEN METEORITE PRESS
Edmonton, Canada

A Golden Meteorite Press Book.
© 2009 copyright by Dax Patrick Noden, Canada.
All rights reserved. No part of this work may be reproduced in any form or by any means, electronic or mechanical, including photocopying, recording, taping, or any retrieval system, without the written permission of Golden Meteorite Press at aamardon@yahoo.ca. Printed in Canada.
No part of this publication may be reproduced, stored in a retrieval system or transmitted, in any form or by any means, without prior written consent of the publisher or a licence from The Canadian Copyright Licensing Agency (Access Copyright). For an Access Copyright licence, visit www.accesscopyright.ca or call toll free to 1-800-893-5777.
Cover art Andy Philpotts.
Published by Golden Meteorite Press.
Post Office Box 1223, Station Main,
Edmonton, Alberta, Canada. T5B 2W4
Telephone: 780-378-0063

ISBN 978-1-897472-05-7

Library and Archives Canada Cataloguing in Publication

Noden, Dax, 1975-
    Poetic thoughts of schizophrenia / Dax Noden. Poems.
ISBN 978-1-897472-05-7

    1. Schizophrenia--Poetry. I. Title.

PS8627.O32 P63 2009   C811'.6   C2009-900350-3

Dedicated to:

Grandma Mildred C. Noden
and
Grandma Muriel L. Bascom

Acknowledgements:

Thanks to Donna Walker for the initial typing of the first manuscript, to my mother for the funding of this project, to my father for his support every day, and a special thank you to my friend Austin for getting my first book into print.

Forward

Strawberry blonde hair, startling sky blue eyes, average build and picture perfect features. Dax's physical attributes are as good as it gets. But that is not even the least of what's truly remarkable about this amazing young man. The eyes are the windows to the soul, and when you look into Dax's eyes you see a soul that is as old, and wise and tender as Father Time himself.

Dax's: tenderness, compassion, love of man and wisdom far belie his tender 34 years of age. His love of nature, his fellow man, his adoring family and of course all of God's heavenly creatures come across in every word, action and caring glance that Dax graces our world with. He is one of the kindest, most sincere, dearest men I have ever had the pleasure of knowing.

Dax has been a horrendous victim of schizophrenia all of his life. From the very tender age of two years old, was when he first experienced terrifying ghouls and goblins floating above his bed. Barely able to talk, he knew even then that something was not right with his world.

All of his life he was hit time and time again with visions of aliens in his room coming to abduct him from his loving family. Cruel and taunting voices always telling how worthless he was, that he should kill himself and put everyone out of their misery. With these horrific visions and voices came black waves of feelings of depression and despair, knocking the spirit and will out of him to fight back to survive.

As a result, Dax attempted suicide ten times before the age of fifteen. He would drink anything poisonous. Cleaning fluids, rubbing alcohol, or downing whole bottles of pills trying to escape the misery he endured.

To the credit of: his mom and, dad, and his brothers Jay, Geoff, and Locke, his family never gave up on him. Life became a continuous door of doctors, hospitals, and emergency rooms.

In spite of the emotional turmoil, Dax completed five years of formal violin lessons. He was voted as the most improved player by his team mates, and was awarded several medals for Soccer.

Struggling with Tourettes Syndrome, and trying to cope with mental illness, he was hospitalized at seventeen for almost a year. Dax turned to writing poetry at the age of eighteen as a release and method of venting his tender thoughts. Dax's poetry tells his story in heartwarming simplicity that will touch the heart of any man.

Dax is doing well now, as the demons that victimized him all his life have now gone into hiding.

He loves writing poetry and would now like to further pursue his career with song writing. He has much to say, this young man and speaks from the most intimate experience. I suggest we all sit up and listen to what this incredible young man has to say.

I feel very fortunate to call this young man my friend.

Donna Marie Walker
[former Executive Director of the Schizophrenia Society of Alberta]

For Me (201)

When two people meet
It may be right
When two people meet
They may see the light

When is a good time to talk about it ?

How do I know
When I should go on the trip
When should I tell her how I feel
Why is it hard to start a relationship
Why can't two people get together
Like in the movies

I would like to find out
If I'd like to marry her one day
Please God, let her be the one for me

For My Mom (202)

For my mom
Who loves me so
For my mom
Who loves us all

She cares for everyone
Who needs to be loved
She'll hug someone
When they're lonesome

She plays the organ at times
And I love it when she does
She loves the cats
And loves the dogs
She loves the ones
Who need to boast

I will love her
Forever
I hope she knows
How much she means to me

Thank you
For being my mom

A Prayer From Me (203)

As I look through the window
Of this tower so high
I think I am lonely
And then start to cry

I've prayed for a life
With love from a wife
And dreamed of a daughter
And son

My hopes and my dreams
I pray will come true
And love will come round
Forever "I do "

End To Dove, God (204)

God, mend my heart
I feel far apart
From all the people here

Lost my faith
I found the wraith
Under a rock somehow

Give me life again, today
For my life feels far away
Lost my way, but I'm here to stay
So I say "Hooray"

Give me time to love someone
Don't leave my heart to bleed
I still want to run
I want you to lead
To the solid reed
I must concede
I have no greed

Now, I'm not
Going to rot
This soul I've got
I still have a shot
And that means a lot

Life begins
With love and sins
When should we learn to grin
For the day that comes within
To rid us all from sin
And keep them in the metal tin

But, don't worry
Life will scurry
Under the door
Open the door
Let the ONE in

As I close this prelude
Will end up in the mind
With a big loud THUD
From the one, whose GOD

Enter The World (205)

Enter the world of dirt
To make it clean and unhurt
We must make it work
So others can see the beauty

Be sure to learn
What you can
And understand
It all is grand

And when you trash
This world of ours
Remember
It's not just yours
It's everyone's

Zig Zag (206)

Move
From side to side
You won't lose
Just go for a ride

Let your feet
Control your destiny
Side, side, forward, back, it's neat
In large and tiny
Feats

Let your body relax
And start again
Listen to the sax
And count to ten

Once you try
You'll want to sigh
When day becomes nigh

Clowns Break The Ice (207)

A clown
Makes you laugh
When you're down
He rides a giraffe

He blows up his hand
When he plays in a band
And sits on a beach
On very hot sand

People wonder
Who he is
He plays in a car
Doesn't go very far
And never loses
Who you are

Some are sad
But they make us glad
Even if we're feeling bad

When a clown
Turns a frown
Into a funny round
He won't turn us down

Love the clowns
Who make the rounds
And they will live
Through the love you give

Many are nice
Which does suffice
This is called- Breaking the ice

Birthday And Deathday (208)

Happy birthday
Is a happy saying
When a lot of the time
Life is raining

When someone does reach
Their ripe old age
They'll have their
Deathday, one day

Time may be endless
People may live forever
Somewhere
But not here

Give your life
A chance
Maybe you'll find a wife
When you sing and dance

Even if you live alone now
Someone, someday, somewhere
You'll meet her
For you

Between birthday
And the saddened deathday
You'll be happy
Maybe for all eternity

Get Going (209)

Get going
You lazy soul
Get going
You're on a roll

Go towards the light
Don't put up a fight
He will call you
When he wants you to

Come, he'll give you flight
You will know
When you must go

Show me the way
Through the tunnel
When my day
Comes someday

I Am Scared When He Gets Like This (210)

When Locke gets mad
He throws a fit
I wish he would play
With that old ball and mitt

He goes into a rage
When he hasn't done
What he was supposed to do
He sorts of acts like Attila The Hun

But when he's happy
He enjoys it quite abit
When he's sad
That is just it
When he throws a fit
You know not to mess with him

A Prayer, For Someone, For Me (211)

I haven't found
What I've been looking for
Am I allowed
To have fun

God please
Show me a love
For a woman
I could call my dove

I am very lonely now
I'm finding life boring
I'm finding it hard
I find I'm wearing
With time

I know I'm young
But I can't wait
I hate being lonely

I need a love
In my life
I need to find
A wife

At least
Bring me out
Of this boredom, please
Tell me with a shout

All Of My Life (212)

All of my life
I've wondered
Where I'll be
In two or three

It seems so slow
All of my life
Until now
Maybe I'll find a wife

I want to be married
In my life
I want to have kids
With my wife

I'll wait and see
Where I'll be
In two or three

Maybe my life
Is changing
Maybe I'll be a man
But, maybe not

Life is funny
It doesn't always go
The way
You want it to flow

Life's alright
We'll all be happy
Someday
That's God's promise

Alone (213)

As I sit
Upon my throne fire
Lust emanates
In my own desire

I need love
To harvest the dove
For me to make
My only love

I cry for love
But none appear
This is my most fearful fear
I fear

Some nights are cold
And dark and damp
Festering old
I make my camp

Lustrous eyes
Embowel my fears
Piercing stys
Weaken my spears

Night is coming
I am alone
Maybe tomorrow
Will bring a rainbow

Brothers Do Things With You When They Can (214)

Brothers
They're always there when you need them
Brothers
Their love for you is so strong
Brothers
They respect you
When you do something you believe in

I did lots of things
With my brothers
I went to hockey games
I went to workout with weights with Jay

I did lots of things with my brothers

With Geoff I went to a Genesis concert
And when I wanted to play a role playing game
He played sometimes

Amber is not my brother, she is my sister-in-law
But I think of her as my own sister
Because she did things with me
We went to have pizza with Geoff and Jay
Locke is a brat at times
But I love him as much as
All my brothers love me
Our relationship is good
We still get together when we can
I hope I make my brothers proud of me
Proud enough to call me their brother

Can I Be More Than A Friend To You (215)

You are a lovely girl
I've never met anyone like you
I am your friend
And I want you to know

You are an attractive young girl
And I would like to be a friend of yours
And more

I'm your friend, to the end
I must comprehend
How to be a friend

If you let me talk to you
We could create a relationship
That would stick like glue

I only know your first name
What could your other name be
It will be hard to tell
I don't know what it could be

I hope you'll be happy with me
I hope you'll agree
Just how it will be
When you're not with me

I know we just met
But I think I need you
At least until we find we can't

When I looked at you
For the first time

I knew I could try
To make you happy

So if you wondered
How I felt about you
Here it is in a poem
That I have written

Let's give it a whirl

So be my girl

At least for now

Brotherly Love (216)

Brotherly love
Comes from the heart
And when you're apart
You know you have a part
To play

Love your brothers
For you must
Because they're the ones
You can trust

Brotherly Love
Is the one
That probably
Counts the most
Even when times are tough
They find a way to make it
Not so rough

If you need to love someone
It might as well, be your brothers
Aside from the rest of your family

Bobbie and Ken, My Mom and Dad (217)

I really love you
So while I live
I will live
With your rules

You're my inspiration
To do what I believe in

When you tell me to work
I will
When I decide to work

When the time is right

If I don't try to try
I won't get anywhere
I want Kelsea to be with me
So, I am going to try
Even f it hurts me
I will try to keep my word
Until the day I die and there after
Which should be a long time from now

Feeling Sad No More (At Least For Now) (218)

No more do I feel sad
At least for now
I thought I would die

People think it is easy
Not to feel sad
But it isn't always

I always feel sad
On wintery cold days
I am usually happy
In the summertime

So I feel sad no more
At least for now
'Cause now I am happy to say
I'm happy, Hooray!

The Goblin (219)

There once was a goblin
Outside my window
He looked so ugly
His hair was green

I was hoping
He wouldn't come inside
I began to scream
As he wisped through the wall

AAAAA!!!!!!!!!!!
Don't come any closer
Don't you dare touch me
You can't do this
This is my house
YEEEEE-AAAAHHHHH!!!!!!!

He touched me on the head
And this is what he said
We're here, and we're here to stay
There's nothing you can do

I jumped out of bed
I ran to the door
He took me away
To a place too far to say

He put me under
A machine
I know not what
He stabbed me
With toothpicks
And very pointy sticks

He said to me
Be Quiet!!!!
Or, I'll hurt you more
He said
You'll be sorry
If you don't do
What I tell you to

I fell unconscious
He kept on hurting me
I could feel it in my dream

About a world
In trouble
Because they said
They were dead

Five years did pass
I have since been returned

They said
We are sorry, but had to get life

I didn't know
What they meant
But now I do

They said
They were making life
For us all

This was all a hallucination
It didn't really happen
It was scary though
Don't you agree?

You May Only Idolize God (220)

Don't believe in other Gods
Because there is only one God
That man has ever known

You may only idolize God
Who is the just, and truthful one
His love is immeasurable
Your's should be the same towards him

God made you
The least you could do is love him
I know I do
And I'm proud

Remember, He's Trying (221)

Someone is crying, someone is dying
People are lying, but there is one who is spying
He's someone who's trying, to lead us up there

He lives up so high, above all the clouds
So high, that we cannot see him
There are people who care, and those that would stare
There's someone waiting for us to come there

Try to be good, and do what you should
And soon there will be a place for us to go
Remember God's words, he promised us here
The words that he spoke, to all of mankind
But some will be blind

And there's someone who's crying
And someone who's dying
Some people are lying, but there's one
Who is spying. But remember he's trying

The Love Of God (222)

The love of God
Fills our hearts
His love we ought
To know

God's love is endless
He never believes we're useless
We should fear less, in Him
And more of sin

The love of God
Is for us to share
His love
Teaches us to care

His love will brighten our day
His love will show us the way
God will come, and join us here
Then take us to a land so near

A land with no fear
Or sickness, or sin
The land we hear
Will invite us in

Lord, Please Come To Me (223)

I need help
Oh Lord
My mental state
Is making me bored
With the life
You've given me

I want a wife one day
I'll charge no fee
When you comfort me
I do believe in thee

Lord, please come to me
I pray, but no one comes
With out a fee

I know I can't hear
Too well, but
I wish you'd come here
In my heart
So, I'll learn to love
Show me my dove
On this lonesome cove

I need a little help
To be a good Christian
Help me to see your love
To help me keep living

Life Is Up To God (224)

Life comes to a close
Where everyone must go
When God says, it's so

I Know Now (225)

I talked to God one day
I even talked to Jesus
I never did hear a reply until today
He showed what he means to us
By showing me life is worth it all
The hardships and the trials

I know now I've talked to Satan
And I know now that he is evil
He tried to get me to follow him

Then I saw the light
Which must be God"s face
I asked for his fight against Satan
God gave me freedom for Grace
Now I be hatin' Satan

I know now that I want
To go to heaven
I do love my God
He is a merciful God

It's Hard To Believe In Him, But You Can (226)

God works in mysterious ways
He may take someone from earth
It's hard to believe in him these days
But think of a birth
As a renewal of the old life

When people die
We are supposed to cry
There's no one to tell us why
But we should still try

We all have to die some day
So don't get mad at him
He's just doing his job today
So we can live at his place another day
He takes away
To get heaven ready
For all of us

Heaven is a never ending world
So we have to have patience with him
He know what's best for us

I know it's hard to believe in him today
But you can
If you try

Help Us Again (227)

God has promised
That we'll be happy
Some people have missed
Your words

We need to hear
From you again
To stop our fear
And pain

Bring a train
To shelter us from the rain
As we travel to heaven
The way our engines are revin'
We'll be there soon
With the many a loon
The birds I mean

Heaven and Hell (228)

I believe
That all is good and evil
And that when we leave
Our first home, on earth

We have to be good
In order to live in heaven
If you're bad, you'll go to hell
That's how God sees it
How does God look at us all
Will we go to heaven
Or go to hell and rot
Is that all

God Loves You, No Matter What You Do (229)

God loves you
No matter what you do
You could have killed someone
He'll still love you

God loves you
He doesn't mind
What religion you are
As long as you believe in him

God loves you
Just give him the chance to
He'll still love you
Even if you don't love him

God loves you
Because you are good
He loves you even if you are bad
He likes it better if you are good

If you want your life to be enriched
Believe in God, and obey him
As much as you can, all you can do is try to obey him
He'll be happy with you, if you do

God Loves Me (230)

God loves me
Even if I can't see
What is to be
And he charges no fee

He shows me a path
And I follow some way
I feel Satan's wrath
And I am afraid

I don't want Satan
To bother me
This is my rating for him
A big zero for sin

I call on God
To rid me of the devil
With all of his might
So Satan will be out of sight

God will save our lives
He'll save us
From Satan's lies
And he will fuss

God, Jesus, And The Angels Will Help (231)

Angels are usually good
The good angels
Tell you when there is danger
They tell you to stay alert to it all

Angels are friendly
They tell you, you are good
Just listen and you will hear
I like it when they sing

Their voices are so beautiful
They sing about peace and happiness
They sing about the good fight
They sing to relax you
When you're uptight

I hope to see an angel one day
I think I'll know
Who my angel is
I don't know her name off hand

Her name might be Elizabeth
I'm not sure of how to spell her name
But she knows mine
Mine is easy

Life without angels
Would be hard
We wouldn't know
When we're doing wrong

They tell us if we're wrong
We just have to listen

They will guide us
To eternity

Let your angel guide you
They love you
They want you to live long
That's what you have to do

We all need the guidance
So keep them in your life
Keep God and Jesus in your life and heart
Leaving Satan behind

If Satan won't leave you
Ask God, Jesus, and the angels
To take him away from you
They will take him away

Make God a big part in your life
Let him show you the way
Jesus will show you
To his kingdom

We will all be free then
We will be happy
Without fear

God Is God (232)

God is God
He lives in your heart
He lives in heaven
We're not far apart

God is God
His love for you is stronger
Than anyone elses
They all love you longer
Than the evil ones below

Love God
With everything you've got
And you won't go
To the place that's not so hot

God is God
He loves you with
All his heart
Just remember
We're not far apart
So, give him your heart

God, I Love You (233)

Oh God
You are almighty
I may be odd
But hug me tightly
Anyway

I love your world
It really is good
You, I've tried
And understood

I've always known that you were there
Even though I've made you
Pull out your hair

Soon you'll come
And live with us
Man will make a big fuss

Some, however
Will love you forever
Many I hope
Will help others to cope
Sliding down the slope

I love you
And always will

Get Me Going (234)

Why do I cower
When something new arrives
Maybe it's the lack of power
How does it keep me alive

I want to prosper
I want to live long
I have to change my posture
To do what is not wrong

I hate to disappoint others
I hate to disappoint me
I want to please all my brothers
Instead of being a flea

As I write
It feels a little bit easier
I enrich my life
I hope not to be lazier

God show me the way
Poke me with a lance
If I say leave me alone
Give me a swift kick in the pants
To make me go on my own
And sit on my throne

God Help Me Heal, I Love You And Trust You (235)

As I wait
I wonder how
How long 'till I'm happy
How long 'till I'm married
How long 'till I am in health's glance
And how long 'till life gives me a chance

As I wait
I wonder, if I'll get sick again
Or if I'll stay as healthy as I am today
Will my meds lose their effect on me

I'm afraid I'll be dead one day
And if it's caused by me
I'll never get into heaven or hell
I'll just roam the universe sad and alone

So please God, help me
Take away my illness
So I can live a normal life
Give me a wife
And healthy children
And all the wonderful things in life
Which you can provide for me

As this song comes to a close
The feelings have changed
Since the beginning of the chorus
God I love you and trust you

God... Is She The One? (236)

I pray to you
For love, and for joy
To bring to my life
Someone to enjoy

I pray for happiness
For what I can give
My love needs to shine
In life I will live

I pray to you God
Let this one be your gift to me
And I'll love dear Stephanie, and her little ones too

A Time Will Come (237)

A time will come
Where peace will shine
Most or some
Will believe the devine

Spring will spring up
And time will be good
Flowers will bloom
And rain will fall

Then summertime
Will start to rise
People will begin to compromise
And good will be the time

Autumn will slow the clock
And winter will climb the top
Life will bring around
The freshly, awesome, and wondrous ground

The time will come
It will all be fun
With all the yarn's that's spun
This poem is finished and done

So read it again, and have some fun

A Life That Way (238)

Pick a spot
Where you will sing
Leave the lot
Where sorrow brings

Show me where
That place will be
That you share your
Your life with me

When I'm in doubt
Don't let me pout
Just sing me a song
That lasts so long

I haven't found you yet
But, somewhere, sometime
You I'll get
You'll be unaware my pet

When you come my way
I'll just learn to say
How much I'll care for you
Though I won't say it too soon

I want a wife
One day
Maybe you'll come to stay
And start a life with me
Someway

Before, My Lord (239)

I can't wait
To go through the gate
Into the world of heaven

In Heaven
There is no pain
No sorrow caused
By the rain

Before my Lord
Comes to me
I must pray, that I will see
The things he lays before my eyes

Lonely days
Will soon not be
Soon it will be busy
The pop I drink is quite fizzy
Sometimes it makes me feel dizzy

Jesus, I love you
Show me the way
Don't leave me behind
That's what I pray

Before my Lord
Will come to me
I will pray, so I will see
All the things he lays before me

Being True (240)

Love as you must
But, try not to fuss
When you're not here
With us

Anger is useless
Especially when
It's someone you love
You have to confess

Don't tell lies
Or, you'll break
Many ties
And you'll lose faith
In yourself

Try not to cheat
Because, he's judging your feat
While you're trudging along
The way that you meet

Always remember
He loves you forever
No matter what crime you commit
Try to be honest
And you'll never
Go wrong
You'll go up to heaven
When you sing this song
This is how
To be true
You'll be happy, with you
If you do

Dear God (241)

Dear God
I hope my life will be a life
I hope my life will be with a wife
Kelsea is the only, one girl in my life
I want to learn to love her, in order
For her to be my wife

Fears Take Flight (242)

Before the light
My darkness came
Fears take flight
As day becomes light

Darkness is long
But light is strong
Stranger than
You can pretend

Light comes
From within
And will
Stop our sins
When the day
Starts with him

World of Love (243)

Think of a world
With only love
It would feed us
And put a roof
Over your head

There is such a world
This world is Heaven
Most would like to go there
Where it may be warm
Even during the snow

God is the one
He is #1
In Heaven there is no gun
And no battles to be won

God promised us this
He will bring us home
We just have to have patience
That is what is meant
Before we go to Heaven
There is
A world of love
That is the promise of God
He gives us re-assurance
He'll keep his word
Why would he lie?
He made up the rule
Thou shalt not lie
I may wonder why
But I'll get over that question
One day soon

Will I Ever Find Her (244)

I ask myself
Will I ever find her
Even if I don't have the wealth
I hope she'll come

This lady I'm searching for
Is a lady I haven't met yet
She will be mine
To the end of time

She will love me
For who I am
She'll stay with me
Forever

Please God, let her come
Let her see me
Let me see her
Let us fall
In the stream of love

I hope it's soon
I hope
I hope

Someone's Lonely (245)

A person
Is shy
He doesn't know why
But, he might die

He's lonely
That's why
He may die
This guy

He may take his life
Someday
He needs a wife

He has no control
Over his emotions
He doesn't think
Clearly, so he'll drink

He loses touch
With reality
And may be in a rush
To make a salary

He doesn't know
How to live
Without someone
Being there
For him

What I would say
To this man is
 Don't kill yourself

You'll waste a life
That you can't get back

It's selfish
And it's a sin
You won't have a wish
You'll never win

But you will still
Be loved
After they stop feeling guilty
They might not forgive you though

There is always
Another way
To solve your
Problems

Someone To Know Me (246)

A man and a woman
Are having fun
With their kids
Under the sun

The family
Is why I cry
I say hi to them
Then in my mind I sigh

Just once
Would I like to have
A life like their's
I want to climb those stairs
With all my cares

Why
Am I the guy
Who always has to sigh
And want nothing but to fly

God show me
Show me someone who will know
And love this guy
So I won't die
Alone

Maybe one day
I'll have all I want
Maybe one day
I'll see what I've got

I am determined

To find my love
No matter where she is stationed
I'll find my dove

Love is bound to come
Show me God
I want to listen
And I will

Someone Please Come My Way(247)

I pray
Everyday
For someone
To come my way

Hoping I'll get married
One day
Hoping that day
Will come soon, someway

Someone, please come my way
To make me happy that day
The day, I'll say
I do

I have faith
In my happiness to be
One day, I'll say
I love you

God has someone
For me somewhere
Someday, I'll meet her
She'll be a special one

I just need
To take my time
And this wish for someone
Will come true

Pretty and Cute Are You (248)

I don't know you too well
But I think I am falling in love with you

We haven't even gone out
But I want you to be mine
I've never felt the same
About any other girl
Heck, I've never gone out with a girl before

I wanted to go out with another girl
But, she didn't like me or something
She decided not to go out with me

I hope you will be a good friend
If nothing else

I want to be in a good relationship
That you would be my girlfriend

If you're not going out with anyone
Why not start one with me

Send Me A Bird (249)

I need a bird
To lighten my day
I need her
To come my way

I am only twenty-two
Yet, I feel alone
No one is of my age
In the groups I engage

Is there no one there for me
Maybe no one cares
I feel I will die
And be alone forever

I hope that's not the case
I hope I can win the losing race
So I don't die with disgrace

I need someone
I ask God
But he never replies
All I have is these sighs
Will love arise
All I can do is hope it will
And maybe I'll get my fill

Love Is Rocky (250)

Sometimes love is rocky
When you don't have the money
No one wants to be yours

When you have the money
Everyone wants to be yours

Love is rocky
Like a ship in a storm
Like a choir singing the wrong note
It's like death, but worse
When you aren't sure if it's real love

Give it a chance
It will be good for you
It could enhance
The way you look at life

Love Life (251)

Love life
It is a wife
It's living long
It never goes wrong
If you live your life long

Don't die
When you cry
Or you won't live
To see the Christ
That wonderful loving guy
Who will stop you
From sigh
And lift you up high

Love life
It only comes once
Try to wipe away the tears
And ignore those fears
Of being with no peers
Change those gears
And love those years

Love Should Come Your Way (252)

Probably
I don't know
I believe that everyone meets someone
Who will love them back
At some point in their life

When that special someone
Finally comes along
He or she will not know it at first sight
But over time they will become as one

You shouldn't look for a wife by looking
You should look for a wife by feeling
Because you will be stuck with her
For the rest of your life, most likely

Love The World (253)

Love brings happiness
To everyone involved
If you're suffering from sadness
Love will cause it to be solved

People are happy
When they're in love
Because of their love
They give each other a hug

They kiss
And hug
They hold each other tighter
And waiting for time to last forever

Love brings happiness
Into our lives
I hope it will last
To the end of time

Everyone needs love
So to those
In the world
I love you

Love Will Come Our Way (254)

Love will come our way
For all of us here
Life will begin again
Without the fear
And pain

The world is a lonely place
And sometimes we fall in disgrace
And lose our face, in this common race
Or leaving us without a trace
Among the stars without the space

Love will come our way
For us here, we will stay
And happy days, will guide our ways
With the sun and it's warming rays
And life will again, we'll catch the train
Boarding now and forever will gain

Before you pout
About this world
Remember Christ, will guide us home
Along the path, along the road
Not so far, that we can't roam
Back to where we call home

Love Yourself And You'll Be Happy (255)

Life is good
Even if it seems bad
Life will get better if you just stick it out

There is always someone
Who thinks well of you
Just believe it will get better
And it will

God is always making sure
You do what's best for you
He'll never give up on you
He's always by your side
Lending you a hand

Believe what I say to be true
And you will prosper
When he calls you home

Be good to yourself
Be true to yourself
And always love yourself
And you will make it in life

Love Is Hard To Find, When You're Looking For It (256)

Love is hard to find
When you're looking for it
Cause you look and look
Until you've found it
But, it turns out you haven't

Everyone finds someone, sometime
Somewhere
Don't look for love
It will come your way
Someday

Don't overlook the one
Who you think isn't pretty
You may one day realize
That everyone has some beauty
No matter what they look like

One day you will find someone
You could start a family with
It's not essential you marry
You can be happy with each other
Forever

Love (257)

Love is something
Everyone enjoys
Love is the thing
All employs

Love is the answer
To many a question
It plays your prayers
In all good session

It makes us happy
When what we feel is good
It picks you up
From the bad old mood

I have the love of my family
But I want to love
My own family, Someday

It will happen
I want it to
I'm mapping
What I want to do
Love is for everyone
Who lives in this place
I'll find a space
Where everyone believes in faith
Love will bring
To the world
What is a wonderful thing

Peace will come
When we all learn to love

Love Comes In all Forms (258)

Love is fun
When you share it
With someone
That's not the only love

Love comes in many forms
It leviates the storms
It lets you love life
In spite of all the problems
In the world

Love shows through
If you
Give it a chance to
Thank you know who
Give him a little credit too

Love For All (259)

There's love for all, in this world
For those who love
Even those who don't

Remember his love
Is measureless
Even if you think it's
Meaningless
But, remember don't stop the trying
Oe else one day you may start to crying
And you'll be wondering how and why
Everyone is given love
Just remember the loving dove
And soon you'll learn to love

Love For Animals (260)

When the first time you see kittens being born
You hope you can see more
Kittens are a wonderous animal
You immediately fall in love with them
And you're getting to keep one

The next time you see the births
You feel special to be able to see it again
Baby kittens are beautiful
They seem to have no worries

You love kittens no matter
What your problems are
Kittens are cute
And they make you smile

When we have kittens in the house
I'm happy more often
Especially if one wants to keep one

The names of all the cats we've had
Were hard to come by remembering
Because we've had so many

I named one Charlie, but
It died, I still love that one

I'm Happy for You (261)

I'm happy for you
And I love the both of you
I want to tell you how I feel
Because I know

I know you will last forever
Whatever forever means
I don't know that life is always happy
But I know that you are that way

I wish for you to continue to be that way
That you've always been
Happy as can be

Continue to love each other
Even when times get tough
If they do

I Will Experience Love One Day (262)

People come
And people go
It's the same
When you fall in love

When you fall in love
You can fall out of love

I'll make sure it's love
Before I make it love
I will experience love
One day

Bring me love
As soon as it takes
Bring me love
And it will raise my stakes

I will experience love
One day

I Need To Know What Love Is (263)

God, are you listening
I hope you are there
I need you to do something
For me, sometime

Show me a flower
With a loving power
To love and to cherish
'til death do we part

I've met two women
In one, I just want a friend
The other for life
As my own wife

The one that I want
Is the one of my dreams
She's friendly and nice
And I don't want to lose her

I need her in my life
To love me forever
Please give her to me
I'm begging you, please
With all of my heart

I Need Some Love Now (264)

I've been alone
Other than with my parents
I want to have one
I want to have a love

Someone who's nice
Someone who's smart
Someone who I think
Is good looking

I need some love now
I need someone now
I need some love
I'll find my love somehow
I'll find my love somewhere
I'll find my love in time

I need some love now
Bring me love, Oh God
Bring me love

I Hope For A Life, Full of Love and Happiness (265)

I hope for a life
Full of love and happiness
When I think about it
I feel lonely

I have this dream
Living in a house
With many dear friends
Coming around for barbeques and parties
Having fun together

My life has got to change
If I'm to have this dream
Of love and happiness

When a love finally comes my way
I will make a life for all to see
That I'm a man not a mouse
So that I will have a spouse
To live with in that big house

I Don't Know If It's Love (I Think It Is) (266)

I love you
Even though we just talk
It may just be puppy love
But it's the way I feel

I just want you to know
How I feel about you
I've loved you
Since the second day
I saw you at the Doc's office

I never knew I could feel this way
So soon
But I do

Good Friends (267)

Friendship is priceless
It helps us to grow
We hold on so dearly
To those who we know

A friendship can blossom
And love can arise
Bringing us a joyous
Awesome surprise

Friends For Life (268)

Once you become a good friend
You know how to be a good friend

Once you start having fun
You know they're no Attila The Hun

When you're friends
You do love each other
It's not the one you need to tell
Men are usually uncomfortable about it
They say "oh Brother"
But still they do
They may not want to share it
When you trust each other
You can become friends
Hope it never ends
Friends for life
That's what your goal is
To be friends for life

Friends (269)

We all need friends
To be there for us
They make the amends
They help us focus

Give them a chance
They will make you shine
Maybe you'll dance
With one sometime

Show them you care
Let them know where you are
If you move from there
To keep in touch

Friends make you laugh
They'll help you with your math
And show you the way
You ought to go

The ones who do care
Don't form a dare
To pull out your hair
I swear

Be careful
When choosing your friends
And you'll have a wonderful
And long trip, that never ends

Peaceful Thoughts (270)

A bird flies
To its young
A butterfly
Flies through the air

The wind
Is blowing calmly
The sea is peaceful
And quiet
You hear the laughter
Children are playing tag
Even the Animals are happy

There's beautiful music
Playing in the distance
The orchestra plays
As night falls

Crickets are chirping
Frogs are croaking
The wind is calm
The water is still

The owl hoots
And flies in the night
Children are sleeping
Away in their beds

Dreaming of what
They did that day

Everything is peaceful and quiet
Morning starts again- These are peaceful thoughts

You May Luck Out (271)

There is a man named Roland
He really doesn't exist
He has a friend named Grand
In his mind she does exist

Roland loves Grand
As much as his mom
They start to play in a band
And they do make a lump sum

They leave the band
And die someday, far away
And no one knows who he is now, and
Never again

So when you enter
The life of a rocker
Realize you may never
Make a name for yourself
But if you keep trying
You may luck out

I haven't even started
Writing music
I think I will someday

I Have Schizophrenia (272)

I have schizophrenia
The kind that is paranoia
I learned to accept it
Rather quickly

I just took it
As something interesting
It's hard living
With schizophrenia
Especially the paranoia

Sometimes I think
More than normal
That's when
I start putting myself down

It really gets me depressed
And it scares me
Voices telling me
To kill myself

The voices
Are my voices
They make me worried
That I may die
Sometimes the voices say,
You are an idiot, you don't have a chance
Give up, give in, and give out
On schizophrenia
I hope it won't kill me
Please God, will you cure me
So I won't die by suicide
I really am scared

This World Of Violence (273)

A man is seen
He is beaten and tortured
He cries but no one seems to care

He crawls out of the hole
They throw him back in
Beat him and kill him

Will we survive?
This world of violence

Think about it
We will make it happen
The good will prevail
The bad will be nappin

A man comes into the room
Threatens to do the family in
The boy is so scared
Goes on to threaten others to do the same

The man molested and won
He had the same done to him once
That's no excuse
It is he who did this to him

A woman walks alone
Three men jump her, rape her, and stab her
They have no remorse
They would do it again

Will we survive, this world of violence

Yes, the good will prevail
The bad will step on rusty nails
We will get through this
This world of violence

The violence must stop
Now!

Dreamy Stream (277)

Flow down through the stream
Everything is how it seems
The stream helps to dream

I Beg You To Live (274)

Suicide is ugly
When you think about it
It is not worth it to die selfishly

When you waste your life
Because you're sad
You might not find a wife

Life is not worth all the hassles
And all the pains
One day you'll own a castle
Without the rains

So before you try to die
Think of all you'll miss
Don't say good bye
Or, all you love will cry
They won't be able to part
From their heart

I beg you to live

Leave The World (275)

Leave the world burnt
And you may not enter
The world that is unhurt

Because God
Intended us to live here
Without much pain
Without much sorrow
And without anything to borrow

I will enter
The world that is unhurt
Because I won't leave it burnt
That's what I have learnt

Life Is What You Make Of It (276)

When you're feeling blue
Like a blue suede shoe
You feel down in the dumps

When you think of it
You could have stopped it

Life is what you make of it
If you're always thinking
You're as low as dirt
You won't get anywhere on earth

You'll think life isn't worth living
And you might even do it

So when you're feeling blue
Just remember what to do
Learn to say "Boo Hoo"
And get over it

The end of my poem is near
Just listen and you will hear
That you are good and nice
You will go far in your life

Walking In My Mind (278)

In my mind
I walk around
Trying to look up
From the ground

I wonder
Why can't I find
What I had,
once behind

God?
Will I be happy?
Will I marry, one day?
Will I be able to smile?

I want to try my wings
I want to give what I can
I hope you understand
"Cause I don't

I want to be closer to you God
I want to see you and say
I totally believe in you
I am happy, you exist
Because I want to see what is in heaven
I don't want to go to hell
I'll try to be good
The way that I should
If I only could
I don't know what to do
Show me how

Please

The Little Demons (279)

The little demons
Come to me
I get so, scared
When they do

Their eyes are small
And black as coal
Their blood burns of
Nuclear snow

But when they speak
They speak so nice
They tell you gently
To sacrifice

Don't listen
To their tone
They really are evil
They want your soul

You must fight
Or go to hell

The Easy Exits, Don't Use Them (280)

Life is a little rocky
Because life has exits
These exits
Aren't for me
And they aren't for you

These exits are deadly
They can cause you to leave
The place where you are tested
For entry of heaven

Please don't use these exits
I want to see you in heaven
Even though I've never seen you
I want to be able to love you

This love
Is the love
Of all mankind

I want to be able to talk with you
And tell you that you did alright
In your life on earth
So please don't use the easy exits from life

I love everyone who reads this
I love those who don't
My love will be strong
My love will not go wrong
After you read this song

Sad (281)

I feel so bad
It happened to him
And sad
That it had to be
That way

I hope he doesn't lose his faith
That things will work out someday

God?
Why did this have to happen to him?
Why did it need to occur?
What purpose did it serve?
Please come soon and take away the pain,
 For him

I know God will look out for him
And soon he will come
When we need him the most

I believe in you God
You will heal his wounds
And bring him peace

My Mind (282)

My mind
Is schizophrenic
I have
Schizophrenia

All these voices
Calling my name
Telling me
To kill myself

It's hard to ignore
When you think
You hear
"You're useless"

Aliens come into my room
I sometimes am afraid
They're visions
That don't exist

Shadows are scary
It makes me wary
They tell me
I'll never marry
So, I should kill myself
I don't listen

Sometimes I think to myself
What's life all about?
There's no elf
I try to figure it out

I come to no conclusion

What's the solution?
To all this confusion
Is it all an illusion?

Please God
Show me
Where I'll be
Will I be with thee?

Now, I've drawn a conclusion
It's not an illusion
Which causes confusion
It's refusion
To the solution of life

Make Them Go Away (283)

Don't let them get me
Oh God! They're here
I shouldn't be
With this kind of fear

Please God
Make them go away
They're rather odd
I must say

I fear they'll come
And I will be gone
Because I once wished
For them to take me

I don't want that now
God I'll bow
To you
If you tell them
To shoo

If they come
Make them go away
Attack them
If they come my way

If it may be
A hallucination
I can't tell you see
If it's an apparition

Please make them
Go away

The Madness is Sadness (284)

I remember when I was small
Everything seemed so tall
When I would go up high on the slide
And having a fear of going for a ride
Toppling down the side

Life is a wonder
When life seems to go under
You must live your life one day at a time
So you won't commit the worst crime
Like taking your own life

I scared the people that mean the most in my life
I didn't have that right
I thought everyone would hate me
Because I tried, and almost died

Gone are the days of sadness
When my mind started all this madness
Still, now on these days of happiness
The madness stays but the sadness
Loses it's effect on me
I am glad
I wish to be dad one day

So if you feel down
And don't know the slightest bit now
To live with the madness
Just remember what I have said
Don't let the madness overcome you

Is Someone There (285)

I wonder
Is someone there?
I take a look
And they're gone

Is someone there?
Or is it me
Schizophrenia
Gives imagination for free

Sometimes I'm scared
When these people appear
And I turn around
And they disappear

When they are there
To me they do scare
I wonder where they go
When I hear them on the stair

Is someone there?
Probably not
I say to myself
In hell they can rot

I feel at peace
And can fall asleep
Until they peep
Their heads, then I do weep

I Think I'll Make It Through This Life (286)

I thought I was nuts
When I wanted to die
I thought it was okay
That I could do it

It would have solved all problems
Thought I
When I was admitted to hospital
I thought they hated me
My parents

I learned in time
That I, Who wanted to die,
Had a mental illness

This illness tried to kill me
But I fought as best I could
Didn't imagine I would try to die
Five did I

Now, I still am worried
That I will die
The way I dare not try

I'm going to make a life
For myself
I want to get married someday
I want to live that way

It Would Make You Cry (287)

Suicide is ugly
When you think about it
It's not worth it to die selfishly

When you waste your life
Because you are sad
You might never find a wife
And you won't become dad

Life is worth all the hassles
And all the pains
One day you'll own a castle
Without the rains

So don't try to die
Think what you'll miss
Don't say good bye
Or all who love you will cry
They won't be able to part
From their heart

I beg you to live
Please, oh please
I don't want you to leave
I want you still to breath
And live as long as you can

When I Felt Bad (288)

Once I felt bad
Twice I felt bad
Three times I felt bad

I felt bad one day
And lost my sanities
Because of my condition
And almost lost my days

I felt better another day
And got back my sanities
Because I got better
And wanted to keep my days

Once I felt okay
Twice I felt okay
Hope the rest is okay

When all things seem
To crumble away
Remember the times
Not being astray

Once I felt good
Twice I felt good

I feel GREAT!!!!!!!

Then There Were Three (289)

Then there were three
All one, two, three of them

Then there were two
All tying their shoe

Then there was one
The one who had none

Don't Blunder (290)

Enter the world of wonder
And make sure you don't blunder

Hallucination (291)

I was scared
Last night
They stood there and stared
But, now I'm alright

Beings were in
My room
I ran upstairs
Because I heard a boom

They were trying
To take me
Away to the sky
So I turned on the lights
That eased the frights

They soon disappeared
My mind reappeared
I was no longer scared

How To Overcome Sadness And Control The Madness (292)

Sad I was one day
And thought to die
Then I thought to myself why
Just because I had a bad day
No way

When any time has passed
I try to make it last
As long as I can

Music is what I listen to
When lonely and sad
It makes me think of what I have

I enjoy my music
And in any mood that's bad
With music it turns really good

I listen to Phil Collin's music
There's nothing to it to sing

I may not have the voice of an angel
But I sing to let all emotions out
And that's all that counts
I hope I can listen to music all my life
So that I will be happy throughout my life

The Paranoid Schizophrenic (293)

Paranoid schizophrenia
Is scary
To people who don't know ya

You think
Others don't care
There are people who do
You just have to find who does
Someone who doesn't just stare

God, give me a chance
I want a romance
It could cause me to dance
Outside of this trance

Friends are few
Because people say, EWWWWW!, It's You !!!!
They don't think it matters
Whether we have any
But we do need friends

God give me a friend
So, I will one day marry
Give me friends
So, I won't wonder
Doesn't anyone care?

This Is Peace (294)

A child is playing
Games with his friends
They're all having fun
This is peace

A man and a woman
Have learned to love each other
They are happy
This is peace

Peace is wonderful
War is not
Help the world
To see what we've got

These are peaceful thoughts
I thought up
I'm happy to share with you
This is peace

A bird flies home
To the baby birds she knows
And never leaves their side
For long
This is peace
Look for peace
And you will find
The best place
Where happiness co-insides
When you
Have peace around
Peace you will
Have found

Everything Is Peaceful (295)

A spring
Bright with flowers
A sunny day
Staying out for hours

A breeze
Blows by
Returning us
From our sighs
To happy, high fives

The sun
Is warm
Causing
No harm

The day
Is calm
Everything is peaceful
In this loving song

Clouds (296)

Clouds
Move
On a wisp
Of air

Flying to only
Who knows where?
And dissipating
When moisture is out

Show me a cloud
That yells too loud
But I doubt you will
Without a storm

Don't worry
About your life
It will soon
Be alright

Christmas (297)

Christmas is a nice time
Sometimes it is small
You don't need a dime
To have a wonderful time

When you are small
You want it all
And if you don't get it
You start to bawl

When you're older
You realize
You don't need a present
You know all you need is a time so pleasant
With the ones you love

If you think only presents make Christmas
Then you've got to grow
And begin to glow
So you can enjoy the snow

Together For Christmas (298)

Here we are together for Christmas
With all the love we share
We'll show how much we care

It won't matter
What presents we receive
We'll just know that we're loved
On Christmas Eve

God brought us together again
For another year
That's full of cheer
This Happy New Year

Christmas Day will come again
Following that year old train
Bringing us joy again

But Christmas will never end
'Cause God's love will never bend
And Jesus our one and only Godsend
Is our deepest and closest friend

Here we are together at Christmas
Our love will never end
Because we're in God's hands
And we'll sing in his band
We'll believe that that sounds so grand
Hold out your hand and life will begin again

Take Time For Christmas (299)

Be sure you take time
To share in the season
To think what it all means
And why we celebrate his birth

Jesus was born
To start the peace
All mankind deserve it
Give Jesus a chance

He will come back one day soon
Hopefully he comes back
To feed us with his spoon
And take us to Heaven

I love Jesus
And I love God
For giving us him
It's not at all odd

Please come soon
I have faith
That he will come

Yes, he will come
Just show him your faith
He will come for us all
All who have faith in him

Time To Go To Grandma's House (300)

Time to go
To Grandma's house again
Time to go
To Riondel today

Time to travel
The long highway
Time to travel
The road the same way

Take time
To go on holiday
And if you like to rhyme
Try this way

It's good for the occasion
When you're on vacation

When you're traveling
Take it easy
And what ever you do
Do it your way

As I Wait (301)

As I wait
To go on my first date
I think to myself
I can hardly wait

If she changes her mind
I will try to find
A way to change her mind again

I hope one day
Which will be fate
I hope it's her I won't hate
On my first date

When I Think of Life (302)

When I think
When I think
When I think of life
I think life is good
I think life is great
I think life is wonderful
Do you think life is this way
I hope you think life is this way
'Cause it is

The Calmness Within The Storm (303)

Sometimes I cry
And wish I could die
Sometimes I try to cope
Without lots of hope

Sometimes I sigh
And wonder, God why?
And then I cry some more
It feels like a war

But then there's a calmness
Within the storm
I feel the peace of happiness
It feels so warm

I feel better after I sleep
I feel a calmness under my feet
I'll live long and prosper
With a little whisper
Of hope

So, if you feel sad
You'll soon feel glad
To be alive, and to sing
And one day those bells will ring

I love, oh God
Like once I'd been lost
He showed me how to live
And I know he'll forgive
Me
And He, I will see
Tee-Hee!!

Open Your Heart (305)

Open your heart, to
Those who are not able to
Open their's to your's

Author:
Dax Patrick Noden

World of Love (306)

Think of a world
With only love
That feeds us
And puts a roof
Over your head

There is such a world
This world is heaven
Most would like to go there
Where it may be warm
Even during the snow

God is the one
He's number one
In heaven there is no gun
And no battles to be won

God promised us this
He will bring us home
We just have to be patient
That is what is meant
Before we go to heaven

There is

A world of love
That is the promise
Of God
He gives us assurance
He'll keep his word

Why would God Lie?
He made up the rule
Not to lie
I may wonder why
But, I'll get over that question
One Day

Schizophrenia Is Hard To Take (304)

Schizophrenia
Is hard to take
You don't know
What of it to make

Before, you thought
You just don't have
The mind to do
What you want

You talk to the voices
They don't go away
Sometimes it makes your
Life astray
But please get help
So, you can stay

We All Need Love (307)

We all need love
You and me
The cat and the dove
The dog and the flea

I need love
Because I've never had a love
Not really
Love can make you sad

Even if you cry
When love fails you
You need to fly
And find someone for you
Again

Flying high in love
Will cause one to cry
Because it's all so lovely
As lovely as a dove

When love comes to you
Take it slow
Enjoy it a little
Yes, just take it slow
Love is not to be rushed
Even if you have blushed
Because if it is crushed
You'll end up crunched
Take your time
And make it all rhyme
So you could be married
For all time

Enjoy Life; Enjoy Your Life (308)

Life can be big
Life can be small
Life can be a field
Or a big brick wall

Living behind the wall
Is not very good at all
Live your life
In the fields of love

The field is full
Of greens and blues
The field may have bulls
That runs you to the wall

Don't let that get you down
Or give you that big frown
Life should make you happy
It should bring you up from that down

Enjoy life
As much as you can
Realize now
Being happy you
Happily can

Love your life
Maybe you'll find a wife
That'll be alright
When morning comes night

Make Sure You Love One Another (309)

It's hard to know who is for you
When first a girl comes into your life
It soon will become two

Two girls you're interested in now
You can't decide who to go with
Until one dumps you

They tell you one is not good for you
But that's a myth
They may both be for you
But you can only have one as your wife
The other as a friend
If that's all it is

People Die Sometimes (310)

This world isn't always happy
It seems

People die
And people live
People are also born

When people die
Some people get mad
When people die
Some people cry

When people are born
Some will die
It's just a fact of life

Most people live
Until they die
Which really isn't bad
Because life will come again

Let all emotions ride
When someone has died
Let the process heal
Or else they could appeal
Causing one to die
It's real

When someone passes on
You should think, while crying
Hooray, They've gone to be with God
So you won't pout for years

Severe Abuse (311)

A boy of thirteen
Wasn't happy
'Cause someone was mean to him
His mother

She'd hit him
If he talked
Without calling her ma'am
Until the day he walked away

He walked from his home
To the place no one wants to call home
A cardboard box
Which he hated lots

The police find him alone
Crying on a bum's shoulder
Who knew what the boy
Had gone through

The police
Tell his mom
That the boy talked o a bum
Who knew what she had done

The mother grabs her son
Leaving the old bum behind
The mom turns a gun on her son
The people heard a moan

The boy died
The mother is arrested
And jailed

She wailed

The situation
Unreal, so was the boy
And his mom
But this can happen
It is severe abuse

Don't hit your kids, whatever you do

Money: The World's Curse (312)

Money is the curse of the world
Don't get me wrong, I like money
Like everyone else
But I don't rely on it

If I had none
I'd still be happy
I wouldn't be able to do the things that cost money
But, I would be happy

Life doesn't revolve around money
But it helps when you've got some, sometimes

Money Just Helps A Bit (313)

Money is the curse of the world
Don't get me wrong, I like money
Like everyone else
But I don't rely on it

If I had none
I'd be happy
I wouldn't be able to do anything costing money
But I would be happy

Life doesn't revolve around money
It just helps a little

When The Air Is Warm (314)

When the air
Is warm
From the summer breeze
A time will come
To us, to please

The time
I speak of
Is special, you see
It will happen to you
And me

God will come
To us and them
To take us home
Where love has no end

Wait for him
And Jesus
To forgive your sin
We will all win
From the love within

Love For Us All (315)

God has love
For us all
For all of us big and tall
And for all who are tiny and small

His love is endless
His love is priceless
His love gives forgiveness
And even though we may not deserve it
He gives it to us anyway

His love is unconditional
While Satan's is conditional
Satan only loved you
When you do what he says

Satan's hell is the worst
I can imagine, how so
Torture and greed, lying and cheating
That isn't the way it should be

Be loving to God
And Jesus, and their angels
Treat people with respect
And try not to lie and cheat
Don't ever kill
Or you could go to hell
It's up to God where you'll go
He'll still love you
But, you won't go to heaven
If you disobey his laws
And don't take responsibility
Of your actions

Adventure is Fantasy (316)

A party of warriors
With clerics, mages and thieves
Learning along the path, that they seize

They come to a tree
With rot, flies and fleas
Alive comes the nest
Those darn evil bees

The party is scared
Their mouths start to quiver
One friend dared, to destroy one or the other
He failed

The mages and clerics
Casting their spells
Destroy all the creatures
And heal all their friends

When finally they reach their goal
Half have died, from the bite of those whales

The evil is destroyed
It's followers too

Wearing their masks
They cry for their friends
Who valiantly fought
But lost their lives
In the lost cavern hives

The Quail (317)

The quail is the bird
That is not absurd
When it is heard
The song of that bird

Her family is happy
Following one another
Wherever they go
Until it's time for a nappy

This is how
Life should be
With a family
Which is nestled
So happily

When it's time to hunt
They wander around
Looking for food, where there is no bump
Singing their song
Which is beautifully long

Snowflake (318)

It floats down
Through the air
Turns a frown
Into a smile

Each one is different
They bring joy
That is what is meant
When they fly

When the snow flies
That's not all that is
The love begins to rise
Around the thoughts within

A snowflake
Floats down to earth
It's for goodness sakes
It's a world of peace
So keep the faith

God made this world
For us all
His love is hurled
Into the snowflake haul

Flowers (319)

Blue, green
Colours you've never seen
All so lovely
The fragrance
Makes you warm, and snugly

Many kinds
Some can be made
Into wines
Some into pills

All are lovely
Wonderful to see
Laid before you
And laid before me

Flowers
 Are beautiful
They are quite plentiful

Flowers
Are for you
And I to see

Enjoy

Keep The Memories (320)

Memories can be good
Or they can be bad
But, all memories are good for you

Even if memories make you cry
It heals the wounds
And they still are good for you

At Christmas time we always think
Of the ones who share your life
And the ones who aren't there for you to see
But, they are
They're in your heart
And if they mean a lot to you
Then you will know they are there for you

Even if memories make you cry
They are good for you
This poem is for you grandma

Life's Alright (321)

Life is good today
Because life is going my way
Life's alright
But how long will it last

I wonder if schizophrenia will resurface
So that I won't be able to live
I think I'll be able to get through
This life of mine

It will be rough
When it starts getting tough
To cope with everyday life
Is to cope with it everyday

If you think real hard
You can control some symptoms
Like the voices and the visions
You can say it is not really happening

When life seems low
That when you have to go
Through the thoughts that plague you
So they won't stay with you

You're OK, I'm OK
Everyone with the illness is okay

Drive Drunk, It Will Cause You To Flunk (322)

Driving down the street
Is a thing that should be beat
When you want to drive
You might not stay alive
If you drive drunk

Bumping into someone who won't be around
If you run them down
People will begin to frown
When ever they see you are around
To do what you've done before
If you drive drunk

If you do this, driving drunk
You may end up in the clink
It will make you think
Before you take your next drink
If you drive drunk

A Man Is Beaten (323)

A man of racial disguise
Walks down an ally alone
A man with a bat
Jumps out to the other man

The man with the bat
Starts smashing the man
And takes all his money
And his dignity too
He removes the man's two fancy shoes

The police are alarmed
And the man is OK, now
Give a description
Of the man with the bat

The man with the bat is caught
But not without a fight
He is dropped to the ground
And tied up, with hand cuffs

He goes to court
And gets the maximum sentence
A sentence of two years
He doesn't care

He'll do it again
To some unsuspecting fool
Then he'll be sitting on
That questioning stool

Do-Rae-Me (324)

Do
A word that Homer Simpson says
Rae
Who is Dan Akroyd in Ghostbusters
Me
Used instead of I
Fa
A word not supposed to be used
So
An album by Peter Gabriel
La
A thing you should not break
Tee
A stand for a golf ball
That'll bring us back to Homer
Do!!!#@**#@!

Canada Day (325)

Canada
Is the place to be
Where love arises
In you and me

Together we shine
Through our hearts of gold
Through the loving soul
In our common goal

I love this place
It shines with grace
I keep a warming space
In my heart

Canada
Is my home
I love it so
The love will show
And we will grow

Our Dear Muffin (326)

Muffin was a nice dog
Now, she's gone to see God
Only today
She passed away

I remember
We got her
It was 1981
She was a little one

I loved her
We all did I'm sure
I'm happy
And sad for her at the same time

We are going
To miss this girl
To us
She meant the world

Good-bye Muffin
We'll see you later
Up in heaven
I'm sure you're there

Jaunty As Bart Could Be (327)

Bart is a young lad
Not a human we have
He's not even a cartoon
And he lives with us at home

He's funny as a dog could be
And as jaunty as Bart could be

Blessed are we to have him
Blessed are we to know him
Blessed are we when he runs with glee

He runs around like a mad fool
When he wants to play with you
How he runs so fast is still unknown
He tears around running here and there
He runs around everywhere

Bart he is a funny dog
He is as jaunty as Bart could be

Work It Out (328)

Work it out
You're not aloud to hit anyone
Work it out
You will find it easier that way

Don't fight
Or you might
Kill someone
Or yourself

Try to ease
Their pain
By saying "please don't make me cry"
We could be best of friends
Instead of foes
Where everything resolves
Our woes

Work it out
You're not aloud to strike
Anyone, with or, without a spike
Just try to work it out
Before the violence starts

Why Is There Abuse In This World (329)

When an ogre
Of a person
Violates another
Human

The Abuser
Doesn't deserve
The right
To get a curve
In his or her sentence

Don't feel
Just because
Of your religion
You have to be quiet
About the intrusion

This world
Is a hard one
We twirled
The baton
And hurled
A huge bomb
On ourselves

Don't let them get away
With it
You have the right
To call them a piece of shit
Excuse my language
But this is how
I feel, hearing
About abuse

Why Didn't You Show Up (Oh, You Forgot) (330)

I could have gave you a good time
I would have done what you wanted to do
But you didn't show up
That made me mad

I don't know what's wrong with me
But I want to try and have a friendship
All you need to do is meet me half way

And if you don't want to go out with me
Just tell me and I'll leave you alone

If you think it's alright to leave someone waiting
Well you're wrong
When you said you forgot to come for the sixth time
It hurt me
I will survive
But it makes it harder to meet someone else

I don't do much
So I may not meet you anytime soon
I'm very shy and need someone to help me
Wanting to meet other people

I tried hard to get up the courage
To ask you out
And you won't even tell me if you want me around

Why Aren't Friendships Guaranteed (I Guess I Know Why) (331)

I wish friendships were
Guaranteed
So that I could be a friend to someone
Through out my life

When I tried to kill myself
I scared my best friend
He never told me
But I knew he was

I believe he
Really is worried
That I may die that way

I can only say
I'm not going to, today
Schizophrenia is so unpredictable

So I take my meds
And I won't commit the crime against myself

I hope I can bring him back
To being a good friend
I don't want to be alone without a friend

Violence Is Scary (332)

The man is shot
A boy is caught
How did he learn
To kill

A country is bombed
It makes us feel bummed out
Will it ever get better?

Why is there violence
In this world
They try to silence
The people who talk

Some of the truth
Gets known
But there's still a lot
To find out

A nice little old lady
Is raped
The man terrorized her
And took everything
Including dignity
Why is there violence
I guess there always will be violence
Violence gets silenced
We may never know
How much is really going on
To those who commit violence
You will be found out, one day
If you hide it
You'll go to hell

Together We Stand (333)

Through our triumph
We see the sun
Rising from the heart
That beats the drum

Sharing our feelings
Can help us cope
Bringing us a ray
Of hope

When times are tough
Sometimes, are rough
I'll lend you a hand
And together we'll stand

The Quest Of Life (334)

If you die, by your own hands
You've lost the Quest of life
If you live your life
The best you can
You will win the quest of life

The Quest of life
Is meant for you to experience what you can
Life is precious
And you need to cherish it

Live your life
As if it were a Quest
As a quest that you can win
Even when times get tough

So, give it a chance
Live until he calls
And you will live forever
In the world called Heaven

The Notion (335)

I thought of the notion, it's like a promotion
It gives you more freedom, than a magical potion

Give your love, and love will be new
Don't try to pursue, the things you don't do
And life will get better, and the time forever
Even if the worst of weather

A thought of this notion, it's better than a promotion
It gives you more freedom, than the magical potion

I thought of a reason, to live, and to love
Just to look outside, and see a white dove
Flying through the air, makes me smile and care
That life is special, and that life has meaning
And in my life, I am winning

Smoking: What's The Use (336)

Puffing on a cigarette
Hacking your lungs out
Sucking in some tar
And getting a nicotine buzz

Smoking
What's the use?
You could get ill
Or maybe die
After 30 years of smoking

It's hard to beat
These ball and chains
Because you can't
Get off those things

Lung cancer
That's the worst
You probably will die
Smoking is a curse

Love and Hatred (337)

Love shines
Through the darkest alleys
Hatred destroys the souls
It controls

Love is the candy
A child loves dearly
Hate is the sin of the world
Which must be hurled
Back the way it came

Love the world
It will be furled
Into this lonesome globe
Covered by this robe
We know as snow

Hatred
Blows away
And love
Is here to stay

Getting Over The Pain (338)

Everyone knows
How it goes
I suppose
That could cause a very long nose

Everyone wants to know how
To get over the pain
Of a heartache
I still don't know

I suppose I need
To look at myself
And say
Get over it you elf

I am learning how, now
Oh wow
I feel much better
Like it is a power

Bring me someone else now
So I won't be lonely
I will find someone else
For me, somehow

One day I'll be happy
And not at all unhappy
Though I may have a day
That might go all sappy
That I'll end up unhappy

A Murder (339)

A woman and a man
Are walking home alone
His brother Dan
Raises his voice a tone

A gun is raised
To each scared head
Dan pulls the trigger
The sidewalk turns red

A policeman
Hears the shot
From just under a block away
He calls for back up

The policeman rounds
The corner
Dan opens fire

The policeman returns fire
Hits Dan in the chest
Dan falls down
The ambulance arrives

They lower the caskets
Wondering why
Dan wanted
His brother and wife to die
Murder is a waste
To all of the folks
Who are involved
Dan did not have the right
To take their life

Drink, Drive And You Could Get Killed (340)

Drink and drive
And you may kill someone
That would not be good
Because you would have to live
With the guilt

The guilt is what will haunt you
The rest of your life

So drink and drive
Because you could go to jail
And spend the rest of your life there

So please don't drink and drive

Don't Destroy Our World (341)

The world
Should live
Forever
But you don't care

Our children
Are dying
And you won't lend
A hand

Nuclear missiles
Destroy us
And you won't stop it
Maybe you don't care
But we do

I love this world
I want my Great Grandchildren
To see the beauty
Wouldn't you want future families?
To enjoy this world
The way we all should

Love is the answer
We all must hear
I hope one day
We all will cheer

Don't destroy our world
We need it forever
Or we will not exist
The way God wants us
Willing to care for all in the universe

All Goes Well (342)

All will go well
And it's really quite swell
To think of what we have
Then sit back and laugh

Give life a chance
It will prove
We still can dance
And puts us in a good mood

So if you wonder
If all will go well
You won't blunder
If you ring that bell

All goes well
When we try
When someone has a fall
To let them have a bawl

They will feel better
Then can be tickled
With a feather
They're mood won't be so fickle

Thanks In Giving (343)

Give to others
Less fortunate than you
And when they cry
Dry their eyes

They can't all buy
The things they need
They cry
Because their heart
Does bleed

When others need you
Go to them
They will help you
Write with pen

The thanks in giving
Comes when God
Calls you home
To live with him

The book of life
In pen your name
Appears where everyone
Can see your fame

And you will get
A brand new name

All Goes Well (342)

All will go well
And it's really quite swell
To think of what we have
Then sit back and laugh

Give life a chance
It will prove
We still can dance
And puts us in a good mood

So if you wonder
If all will go well
You won't blunder
If you ring that bell

All goes well
When we try
When someone has a fall
To let them have a bawl

They will feel better
Then can be tickled
With a feather
They're mood won't be so fickle

Thanks In Giving (343)

Give to others
Less fortunate than you
And when they cry
Dry their eyes

They can't all buy
The things they need
They cry
Because their heart
Does bleed

When others need you
Go to them
They will help you
Write with pen

The thanks in giving
Comes when God
Calls you home
To live with him

The book of life
In pen your name
Appears where everyone
Can see your fame

And you will get
A brand new name

Funny Christmases To Remember (344)

Do you remember
That funny time
We had on Christmas Day
The one with the can of
Foam spray, on Jay

Do you remember
That funny time
When dad drew a moustache
On poor old Locke
I'm really trying to rhyme

Do you remember
The funny time
When everyone got
Jam or jelly
In the bag with that guy
Who is so jolly

Do you remember
That funny time
When I got Locke
That mooner guy

Do you remember
That funny time
When Brian got
That yellow school bus
I'm trying to make the poem hot

Do you remember
When mom had got
Those beaver slippers

She laughed did she not

We had fun
With all these Christmases
And many more will come
Remember these Christmases
And life will seem less dumb

Jolly Old Fellow (345)

He comes down the chimney
Every single year
He brings us lots of things
That jolly old fellow

He dresses in red
With trimmings to his head
And comes on a sleigh, today

He makes us happy
After, he'll be ready for his nappy
When he has finished his run

That jolly old fellow
He's one in a million
He knows how to laugh
And he really knows his math
He needs to, to bring toys to the young everywhere

He gives us what he can
And makes kids happy
To sit on his lap

That jolly old fellow
He's one in a million
He knows how to laugh
And he knows his math
He has to, to travel by night
To surprise you in the morning

Stop Dangerous Deeds (346)

Sometimes people
Do dangerous things
They may run out
In the street

People shouldn't do
Dangerous things
Because they could kill themselves
If they're not careful

If you love yourself
You won't endure yourself
In these
Activities

Don't be dangerous
It could be disasterous
If you are dangerous
You might end up dead

I want to see you around
Don't let me down
Stop being dangerous
Or your family will frown
When you're laid to rest
In your grave
So, behave
OK?

Mr. Christmas (347)

The snowflakes descend
On this Christmas Eve morn
Bringing us joy
Which makes us feel warm

The man in the suit
Of red, white and black
Will offer the kids
What's in his red sack

The tears will bring joy
To every girl and boy
Their smiles that employ
Will show that they enjoy

Their love in his soul
Will bring us much closer
To the goal
Even if sometimes
There's coal

Forever he lives
And forever he gives
Mr. Christmas he is

Life Is Wonderful (348)

You should believe
That life is wonderful
You should perceive
That life is useful

We're here
For a reason
Most don't know
What their reason is

Learn to love yourself
So that you might share the wealth
With everyone else
Just like that old elf

Have happy times
Wear a smile
It could drive you the mile
For a little while

Treat others with respect
The way you want to be treated
That will love again
Even if, now, they're sad

Just realize
Life is wonderful
In spite of all
The falls
You might encounter

Admiring Phil Collins (349)

I love to hear the songs he sings
His music brings me joy
Everytime I play his tunes
My life I do enjoy

I admire him for his talents
His wit, and his heart
I'd love to meet him
To shake his hand
And thank him for his art

Choke Down My Fear (350)

My mind is racing
Like wind in my ears
I'm pacing back and forth
In fear-I'm in tears

I cry for a dove
To help ease my fear
For I need a love
To live with me here

I know I will find
Someone, somewhere
But until we combine
I'll choke down my fear

Treasure This Gem (351)

Treasure this gem
Who has entered your life
Give her your love
And show her what's right

Love her through
The good and the bad
Show her she's loved
She will be glad

Bring her close
And into your heart
Love her forever
Never to part

Dreams Come and Go (352)

The time has come
To enjoy life again
Dreams will comfort
And love will share

Share the dreams
O night and day
With the ones of light
And God will come someday

Dreams are tools
To help us through
To realize a life
In more than a dream

Join our love
Shine the day
Reach for a land
To guide our way

Dreams come and go
As fast as a breath of air
Time will only tell
When things will be well again

Morning Grew Bright (353)

Morning grew bright
The sun was in sight
Everything seemed
To be all right

Who could imagine
Such horror to arise
Which lead those people
To their fateful demise

Hopes were lost
To those who cared
And dreams were
Shattered
Non were spared

Views must change
For us to see
The way God meant
This life to be

Santa Was Here (354)

The night before Christmas
I went to bed early
Left him some cookies
And poured him his milk

The morning came quickly
As I jumped out of bed
Ran down the hall
I knew where to head

The tree was aglow
With lights shining bright
And under the tree
Was a wonderful sight

Santa was here
I shouted out loud
Knowing that soon
I would be drawing a crowd

The family took pride
As they saw in their eyes
A room full of presents
What a joyous surprise

The World at Peace (355)

Wouldn't it be wonderful
To have the world at peace
The world would be full
Of happiness, and the fighting would cease

People are wishing
For a place so nice
They're just itching
To ease the vise

We need to stick together
Through the bitter wars
Even though the weather
Lessens the scores

God, help us to keep the peace
Through out the life we know
Please give us the fleece
To keep us warm, while it does snow

Once we keep the calmness
The peace will come
When the world brings happiness
To the world, we all love